WELCOME
TO
ANTIQUE BOTANICALS I
AN ADULT COLORING BOOK

PLEASE VISIT OUR WEBSITE AT
WWW.BOTANICALARTDESIGNS.COM
FOR MORE INFORMATION ON
NEW DESIGNS AND BOOKS.

ISBN: 1519711670
ISBN-13: 978-1519711670

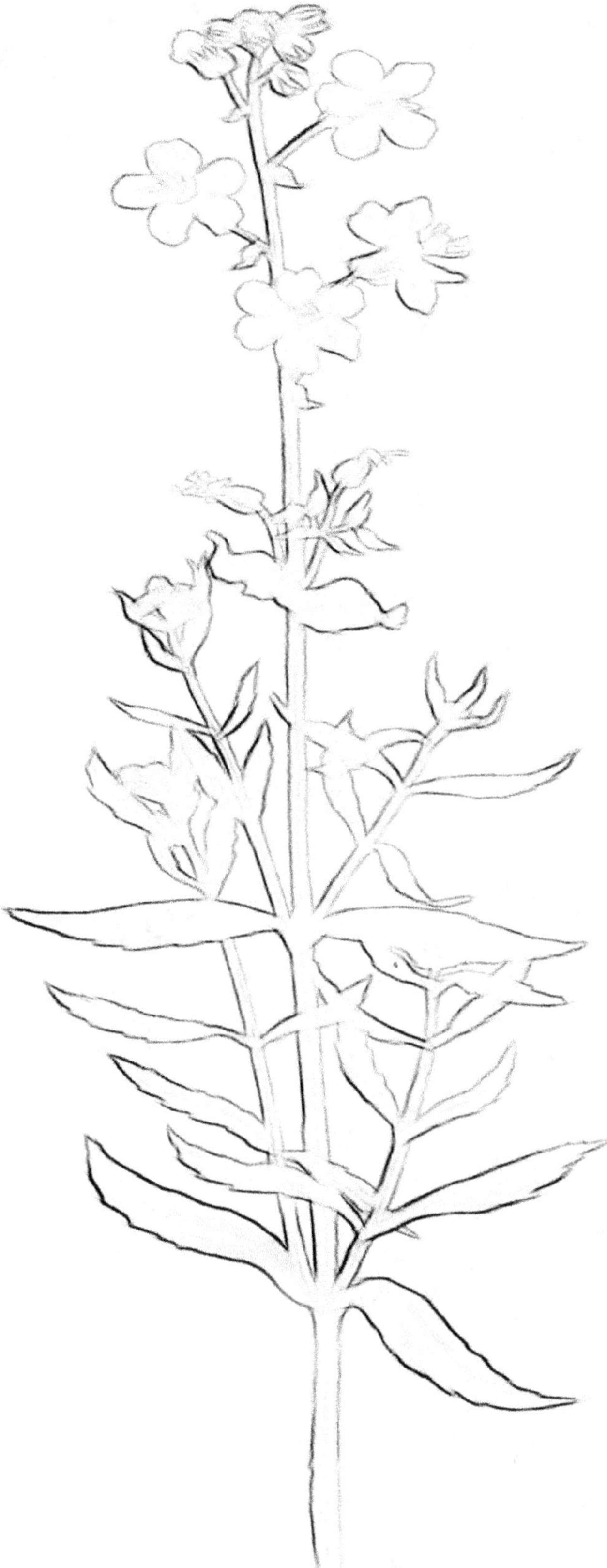

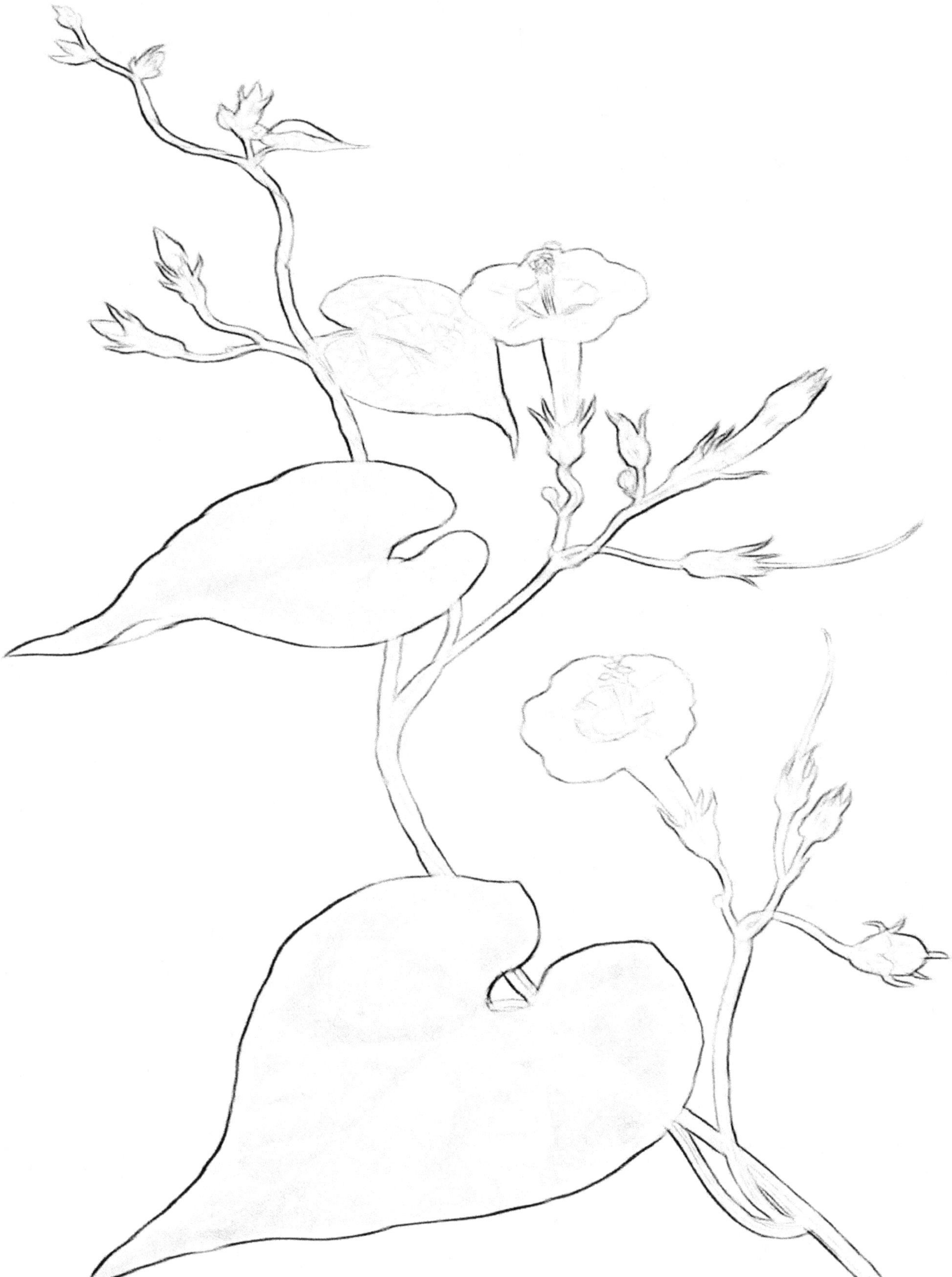

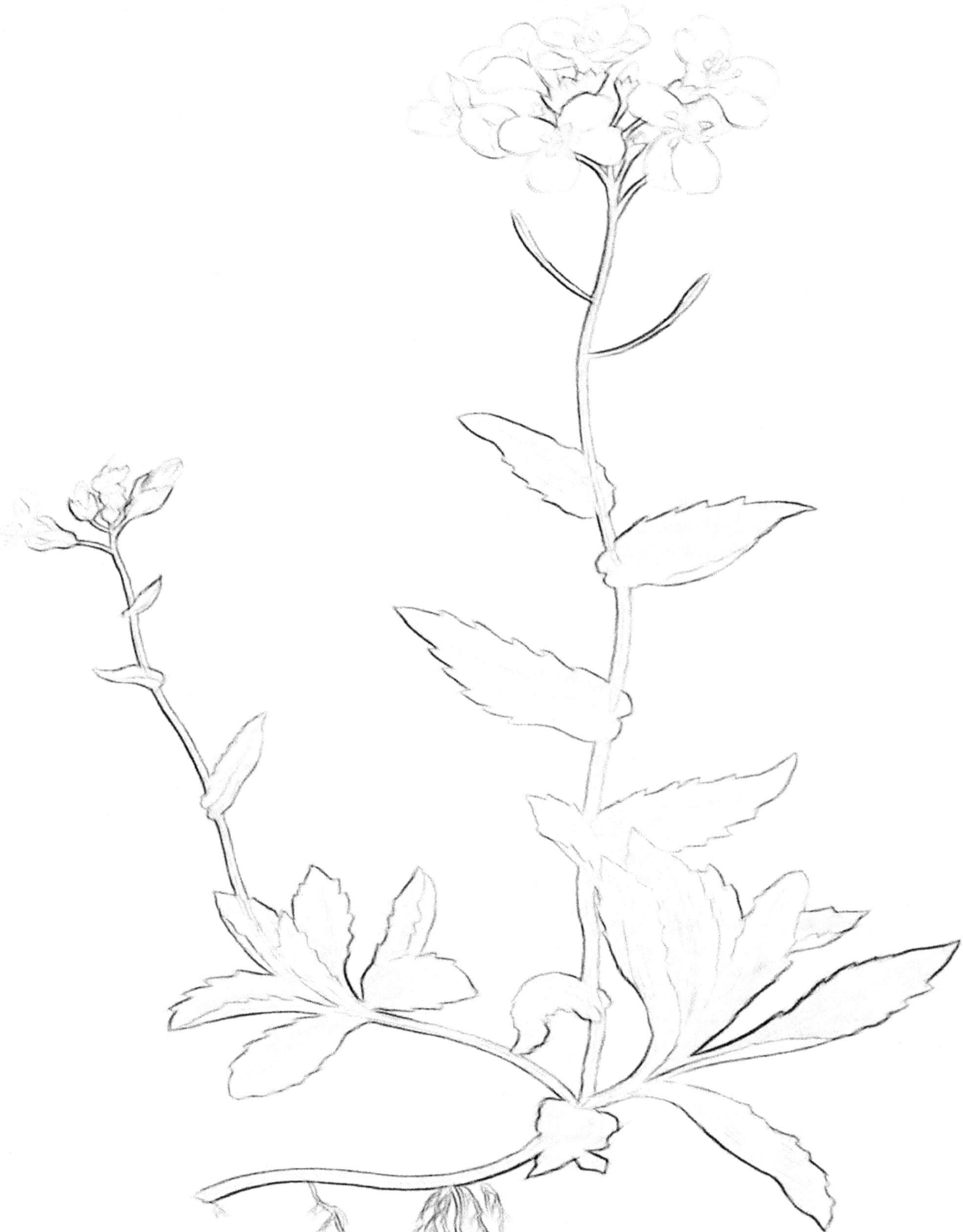

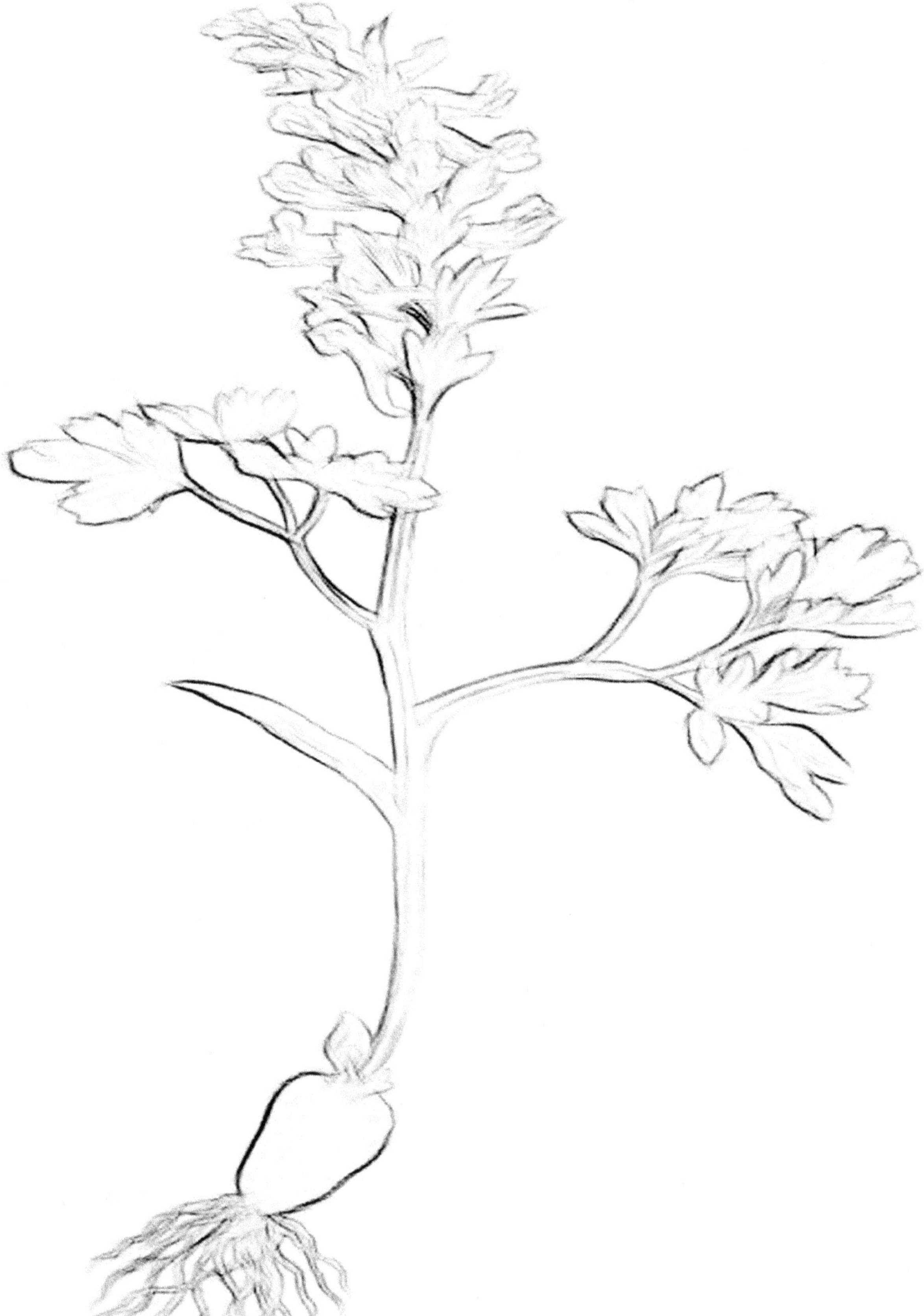

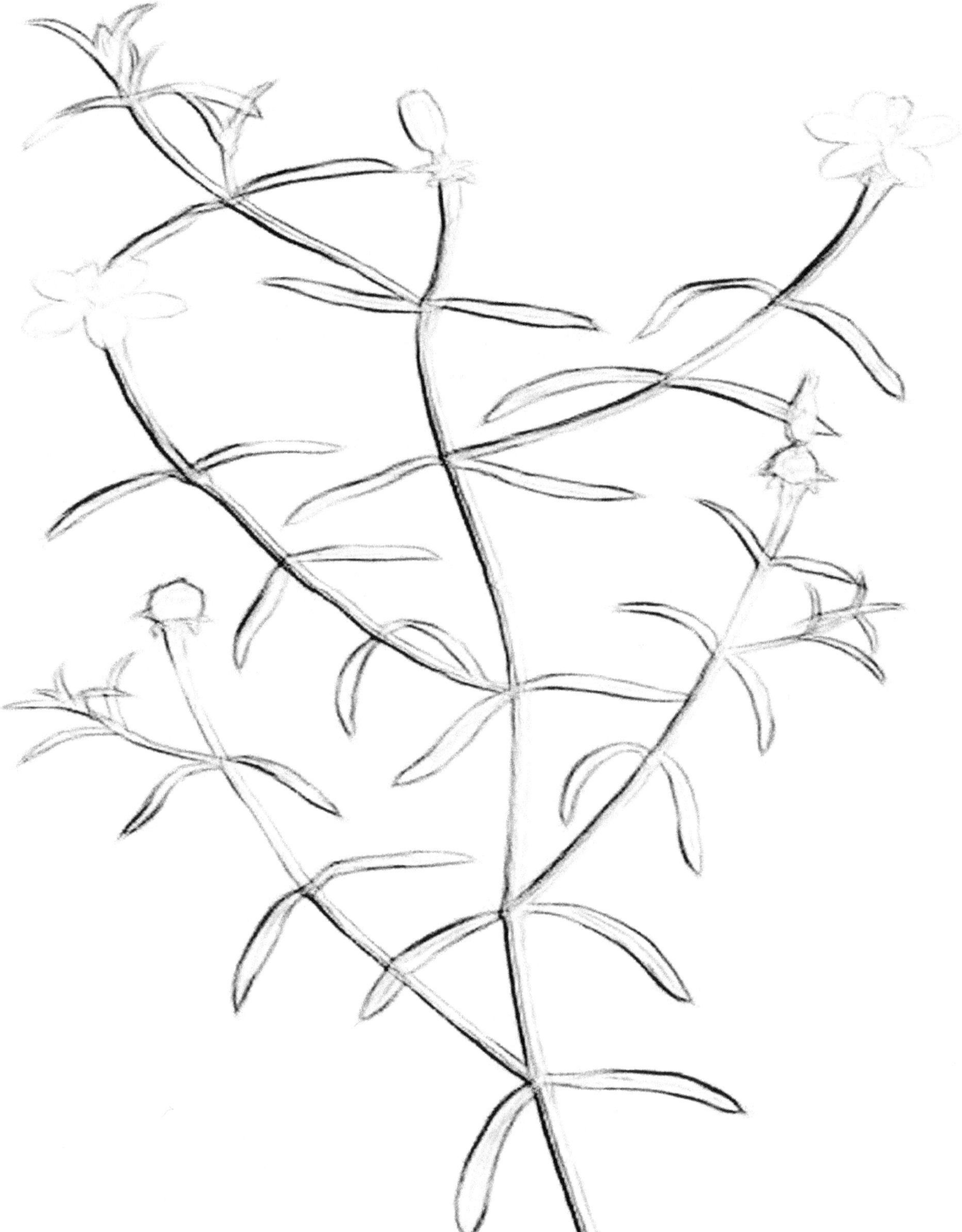

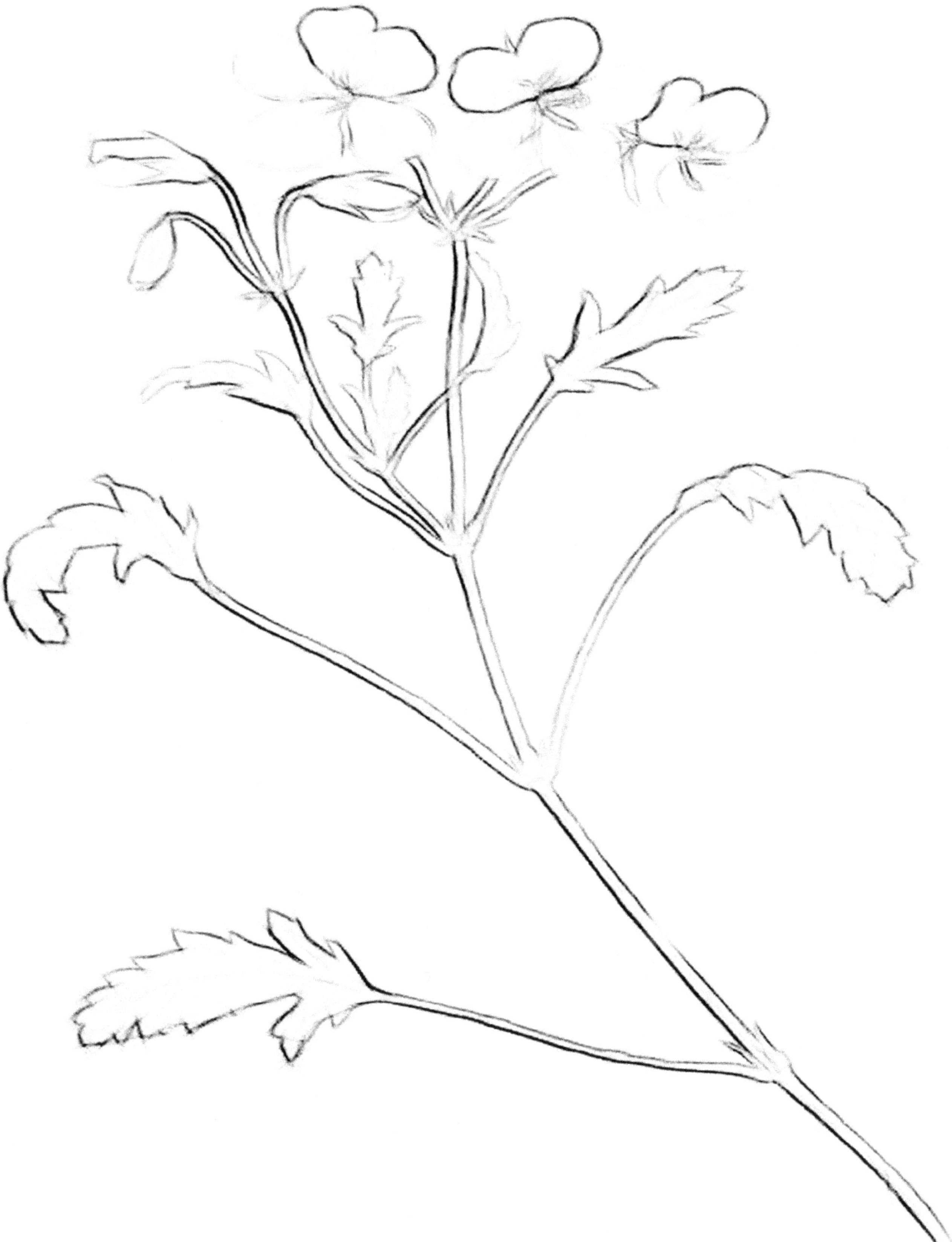

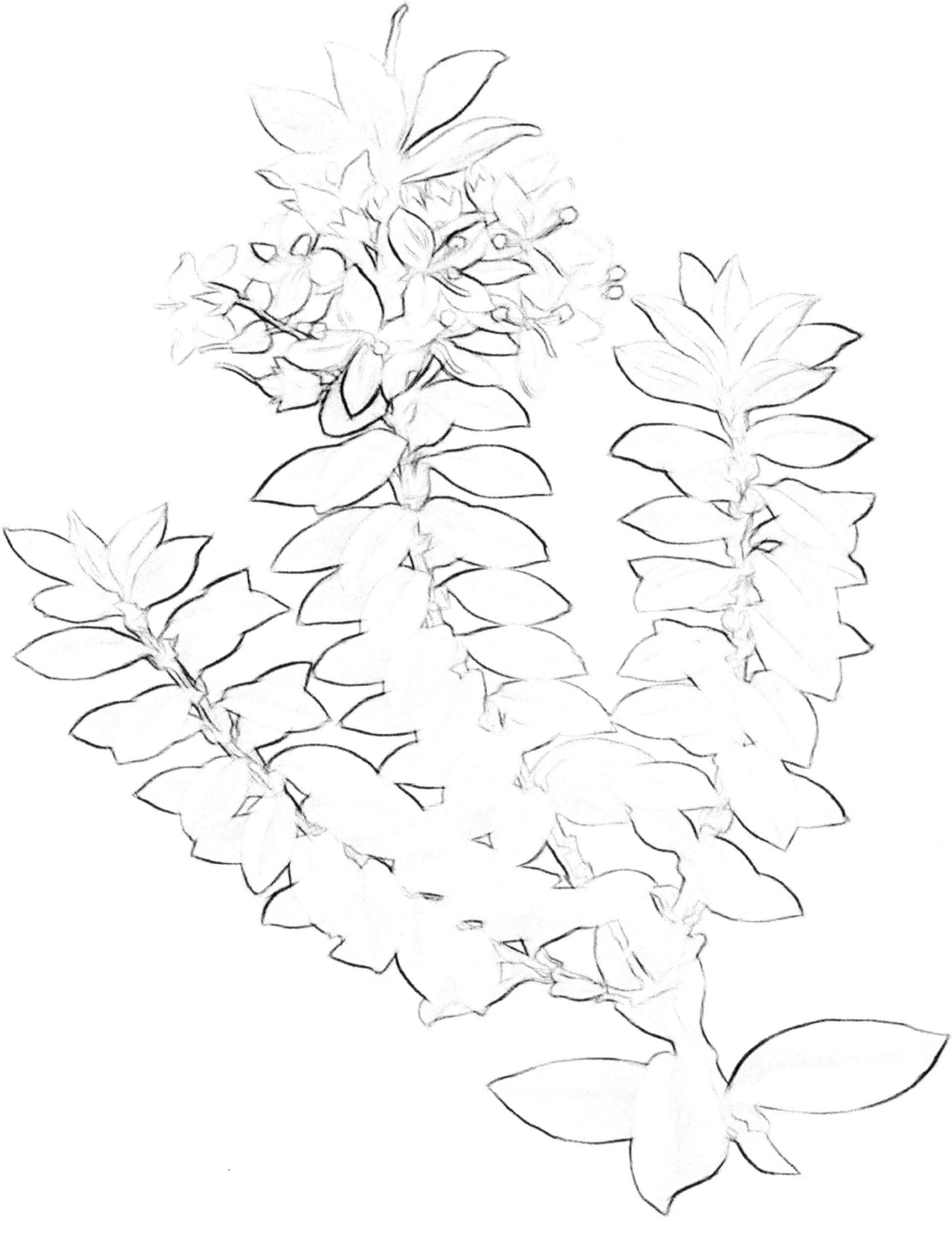

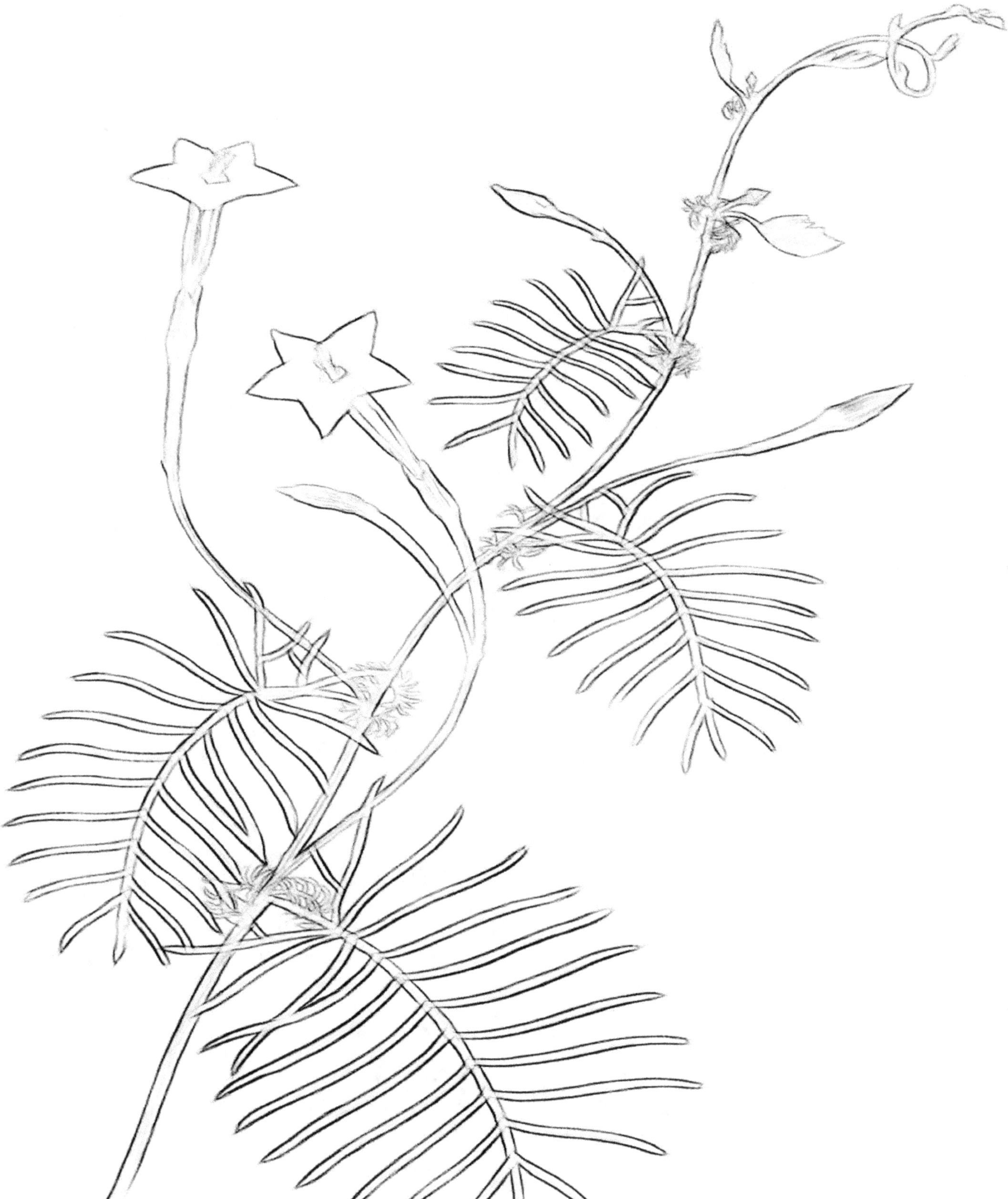

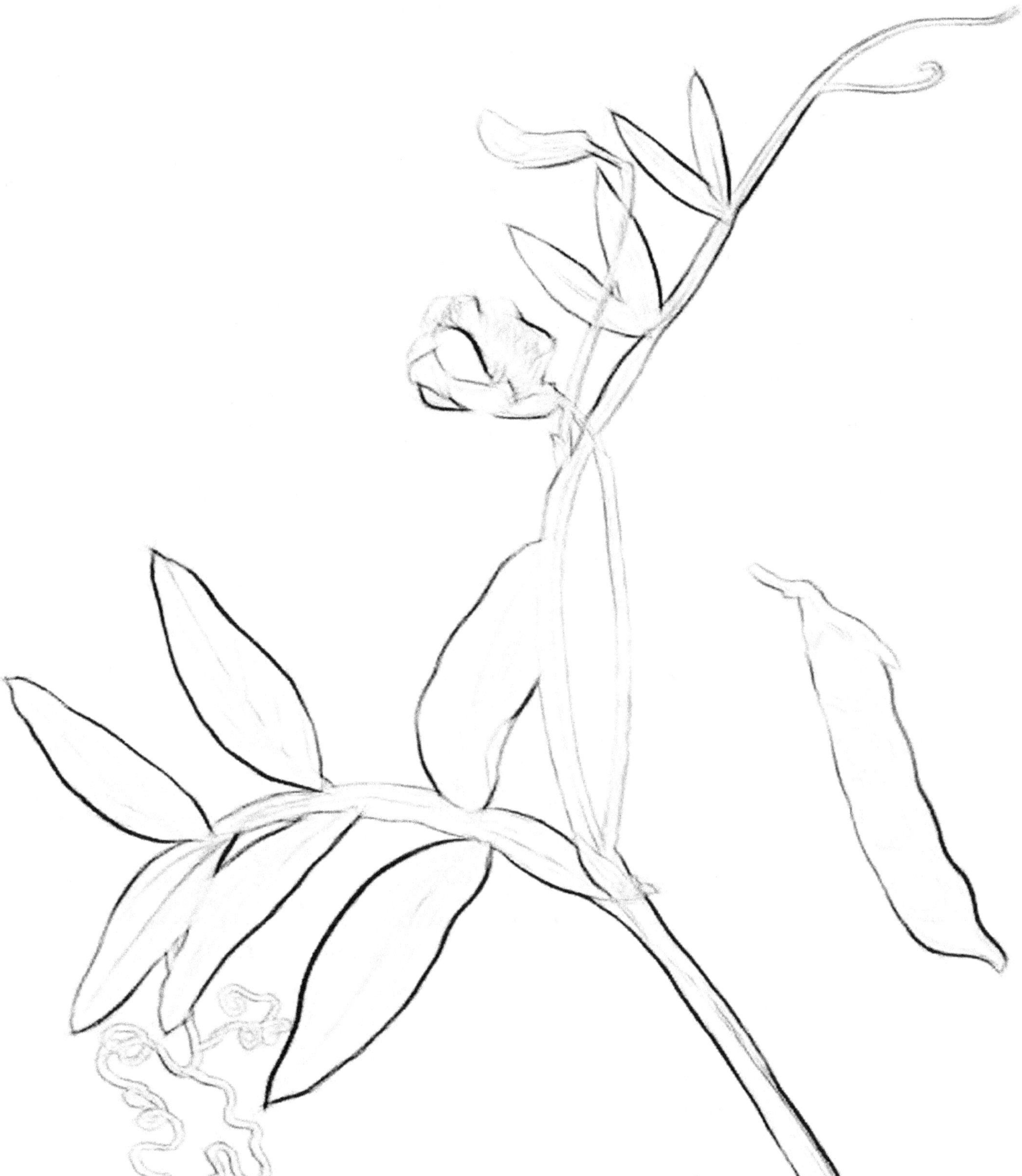

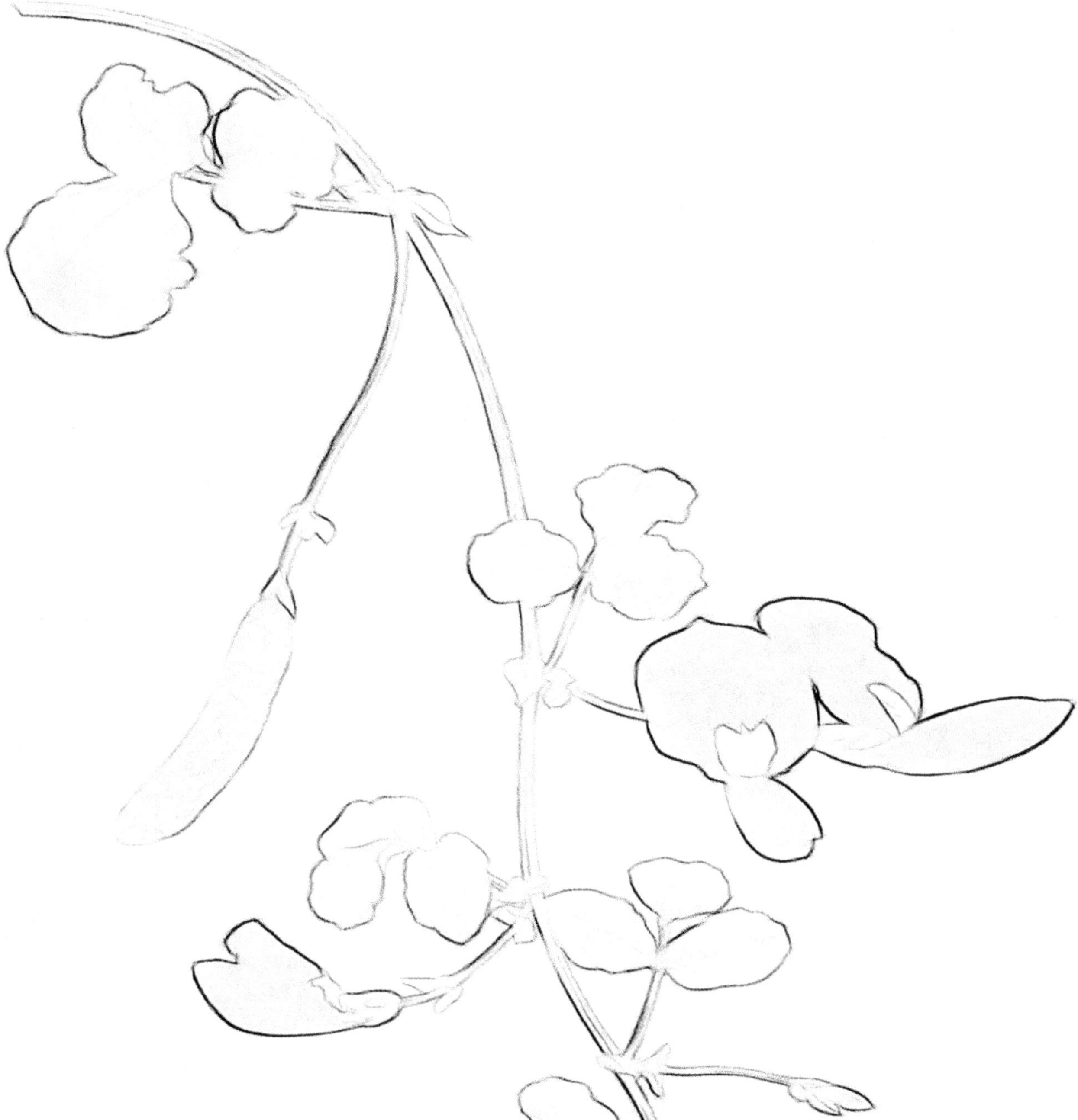

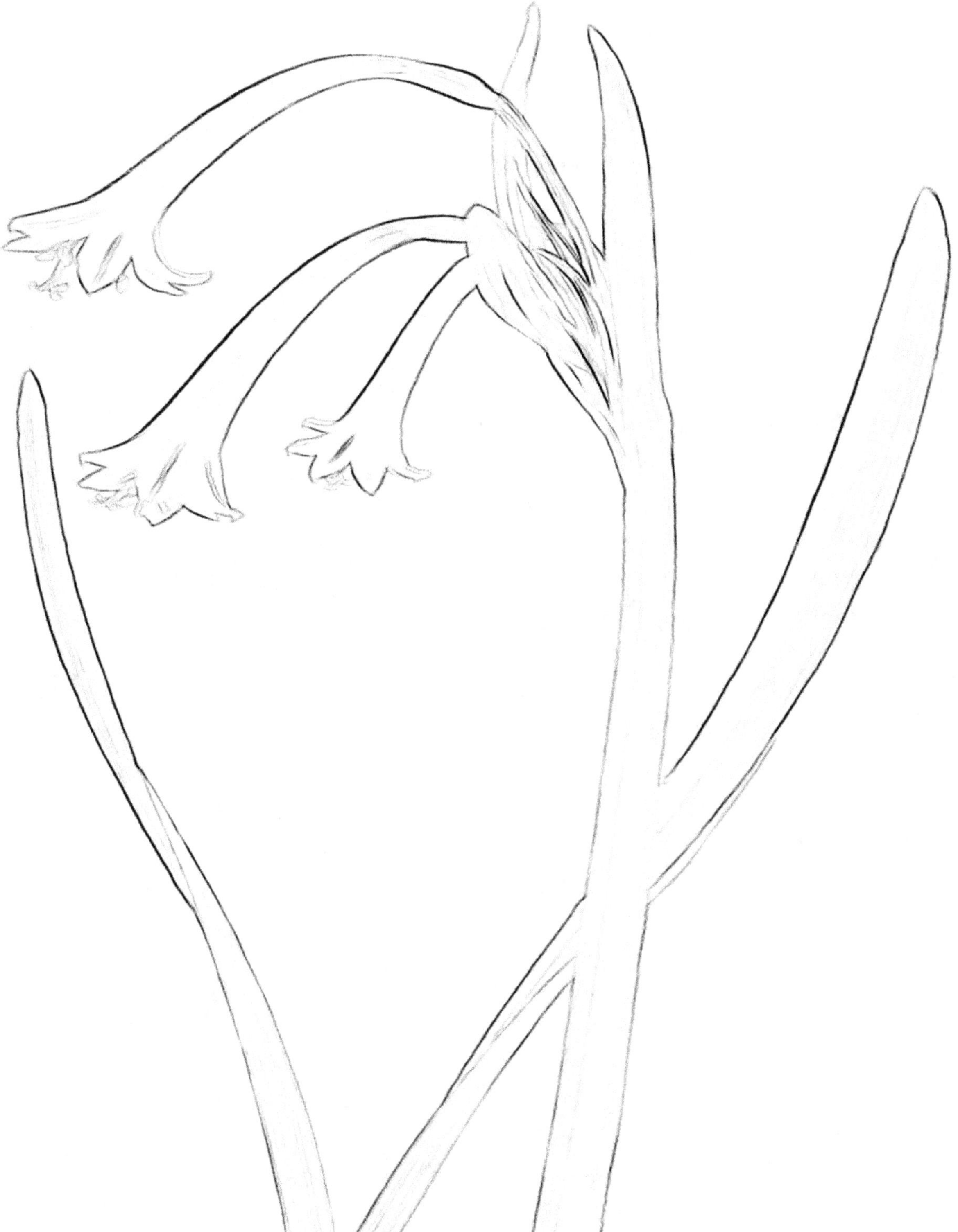

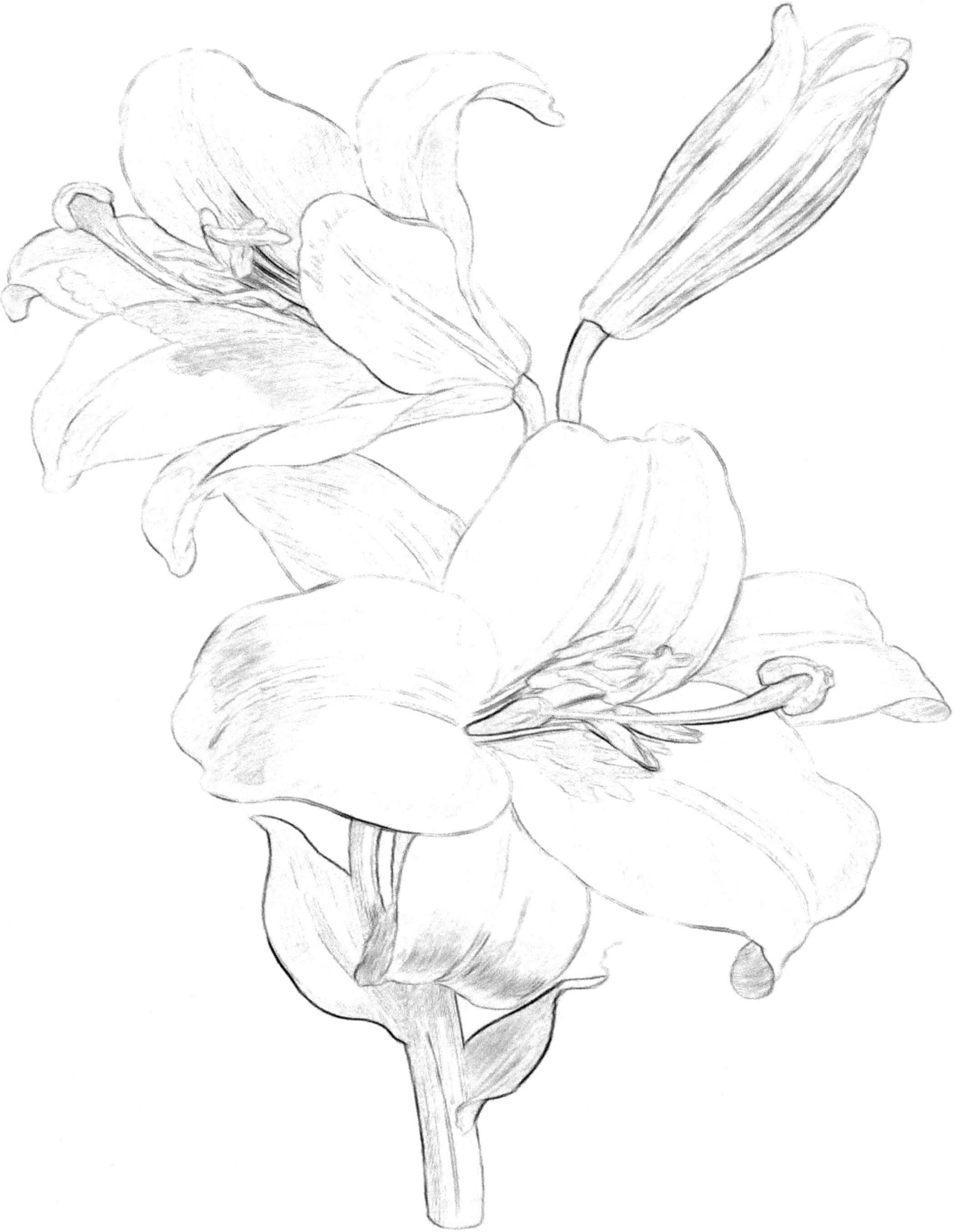

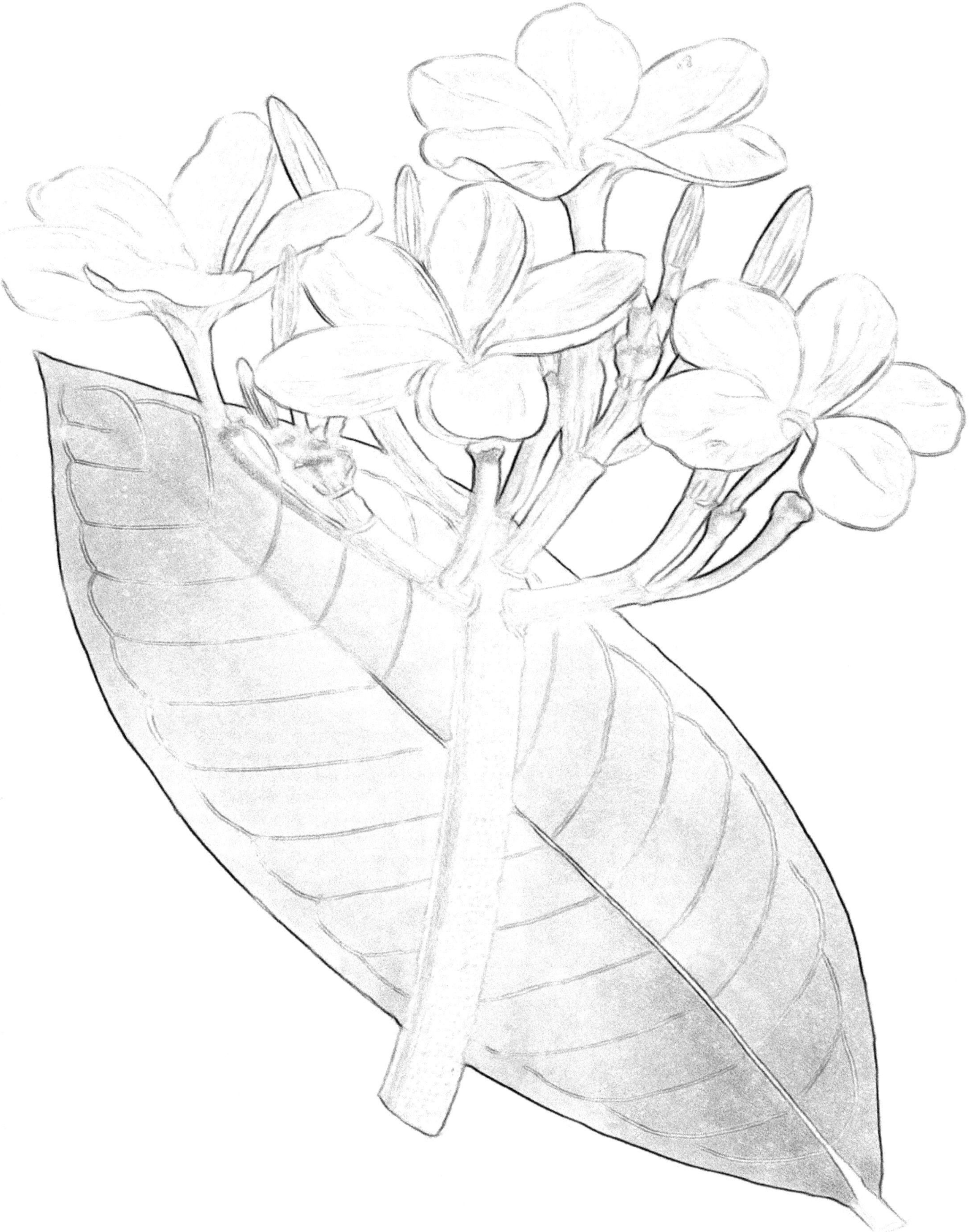

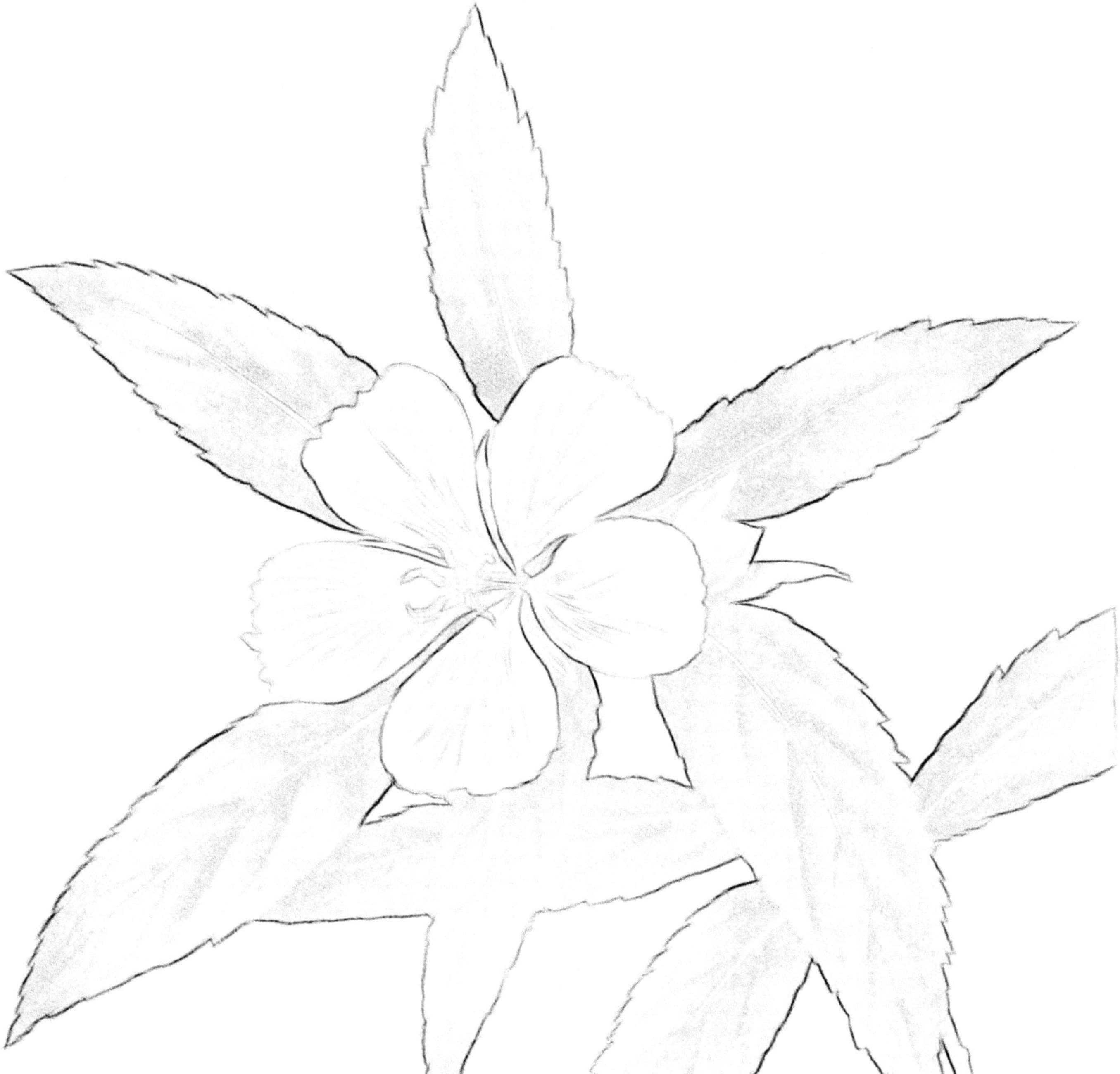

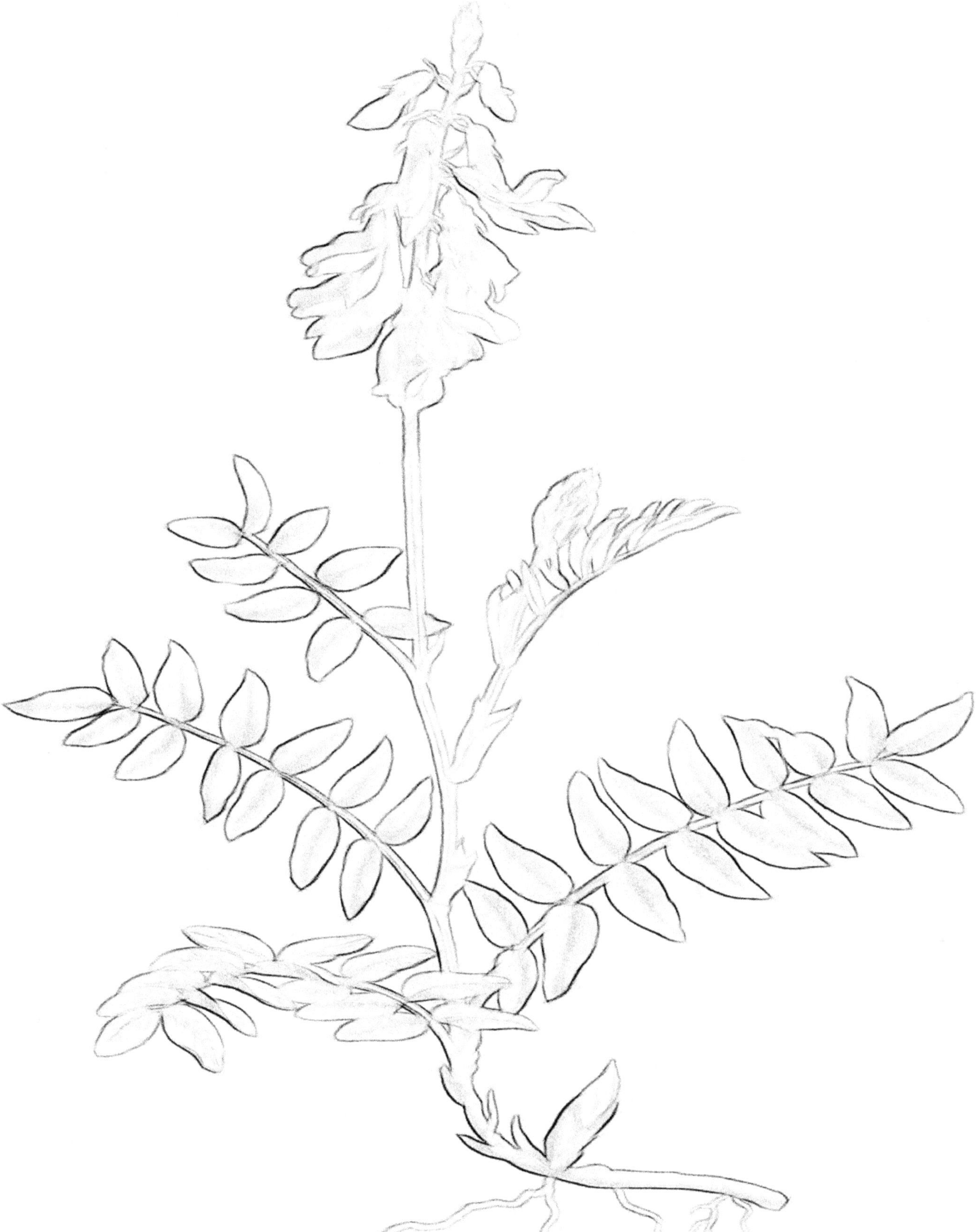

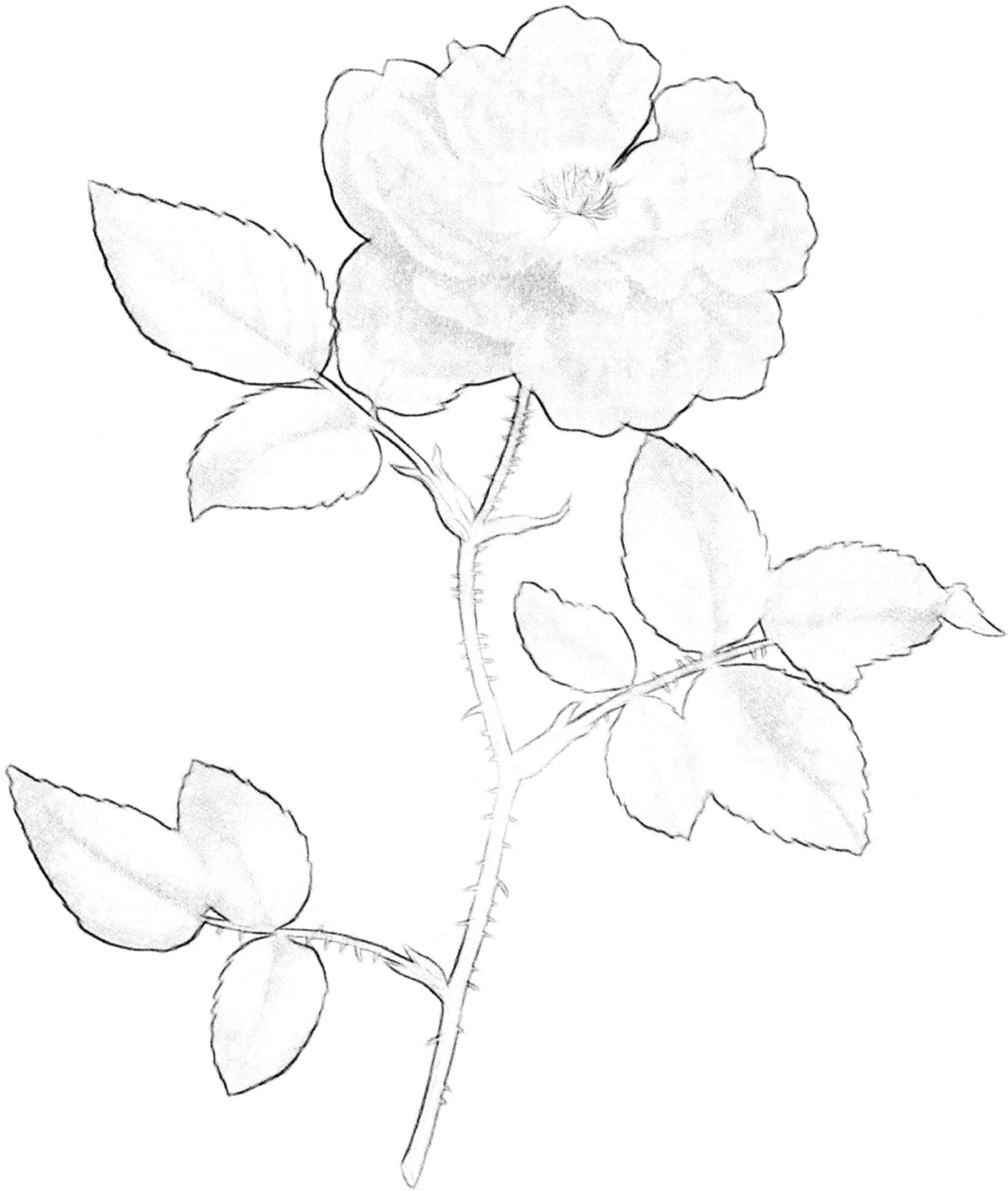

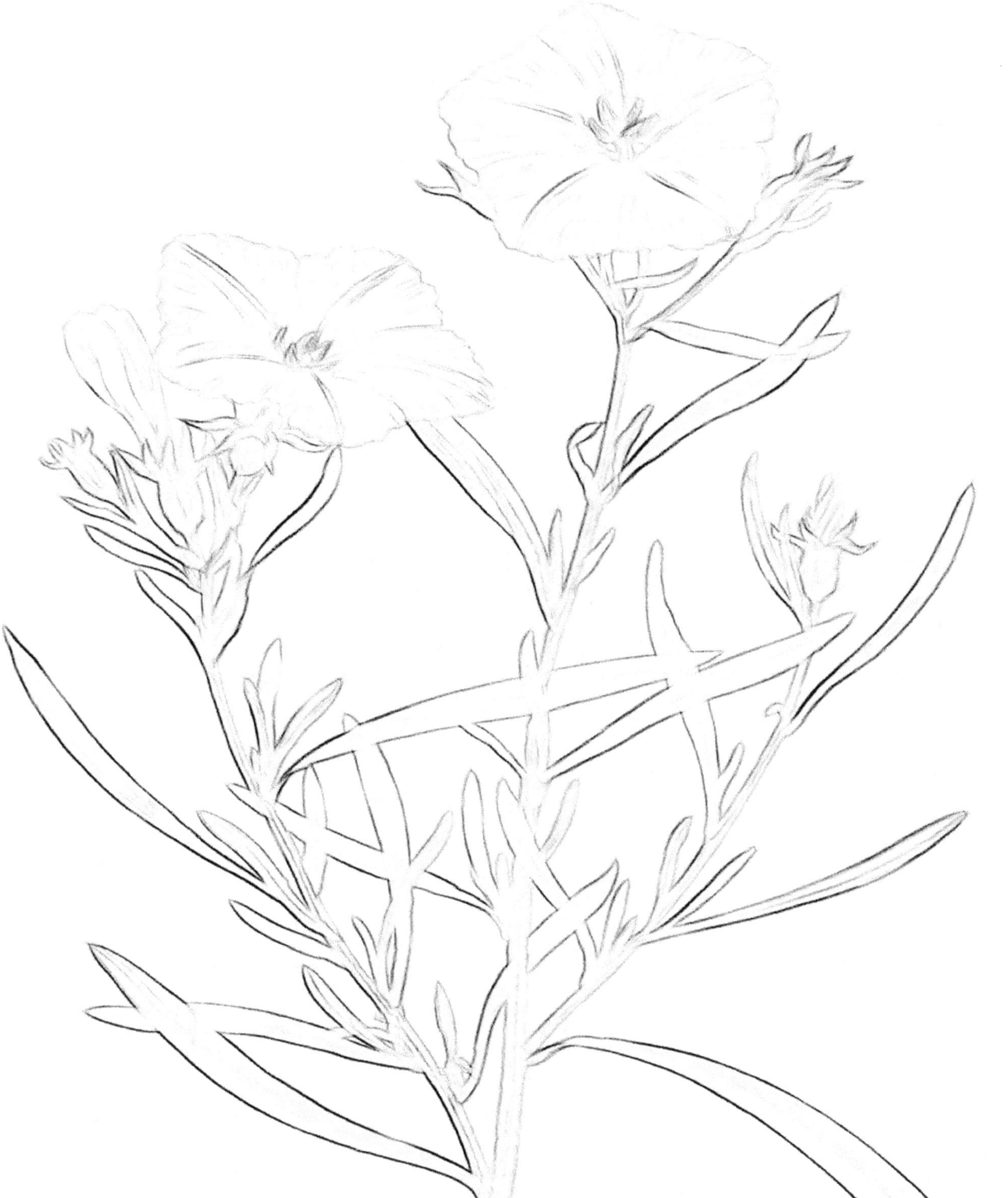

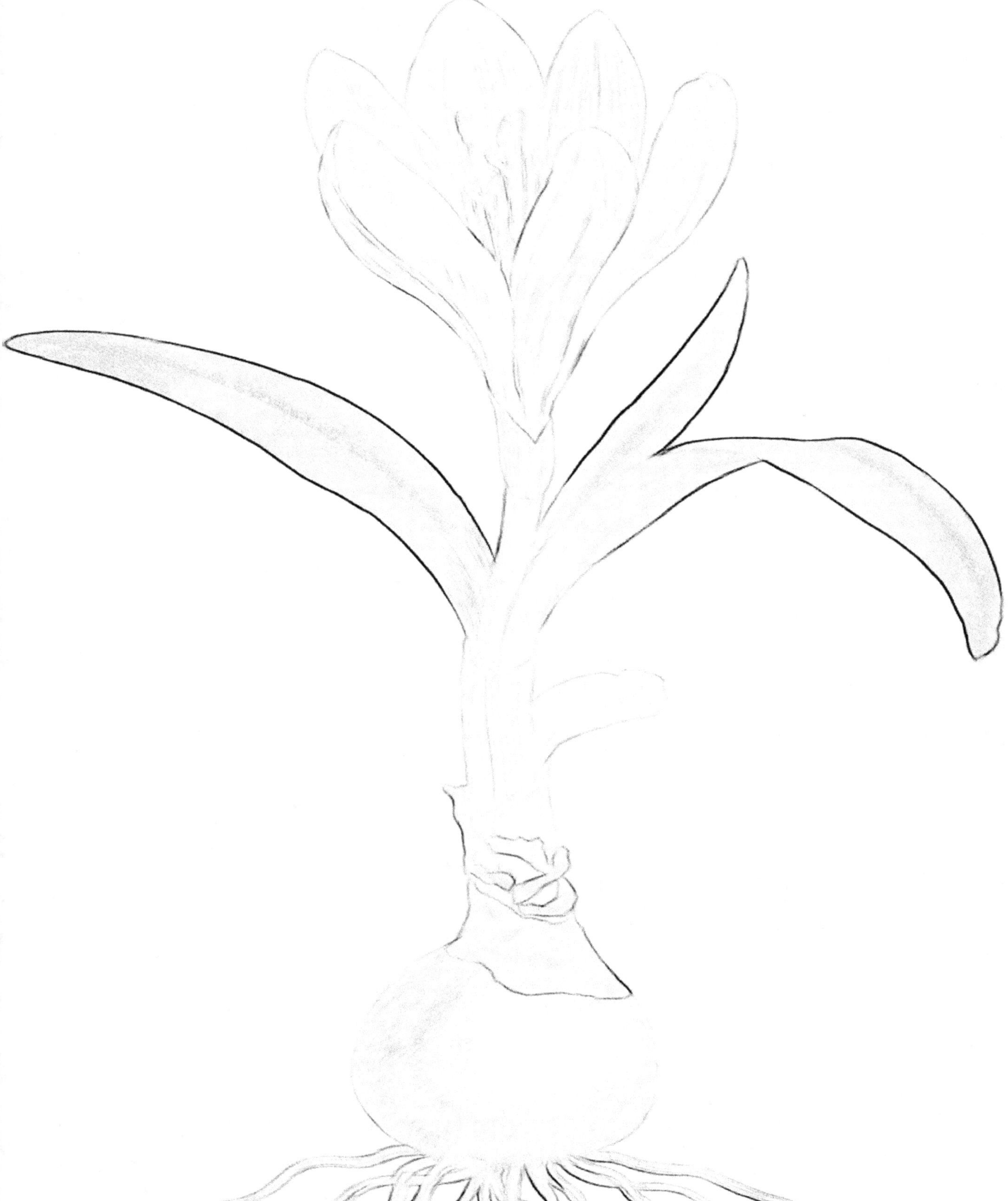

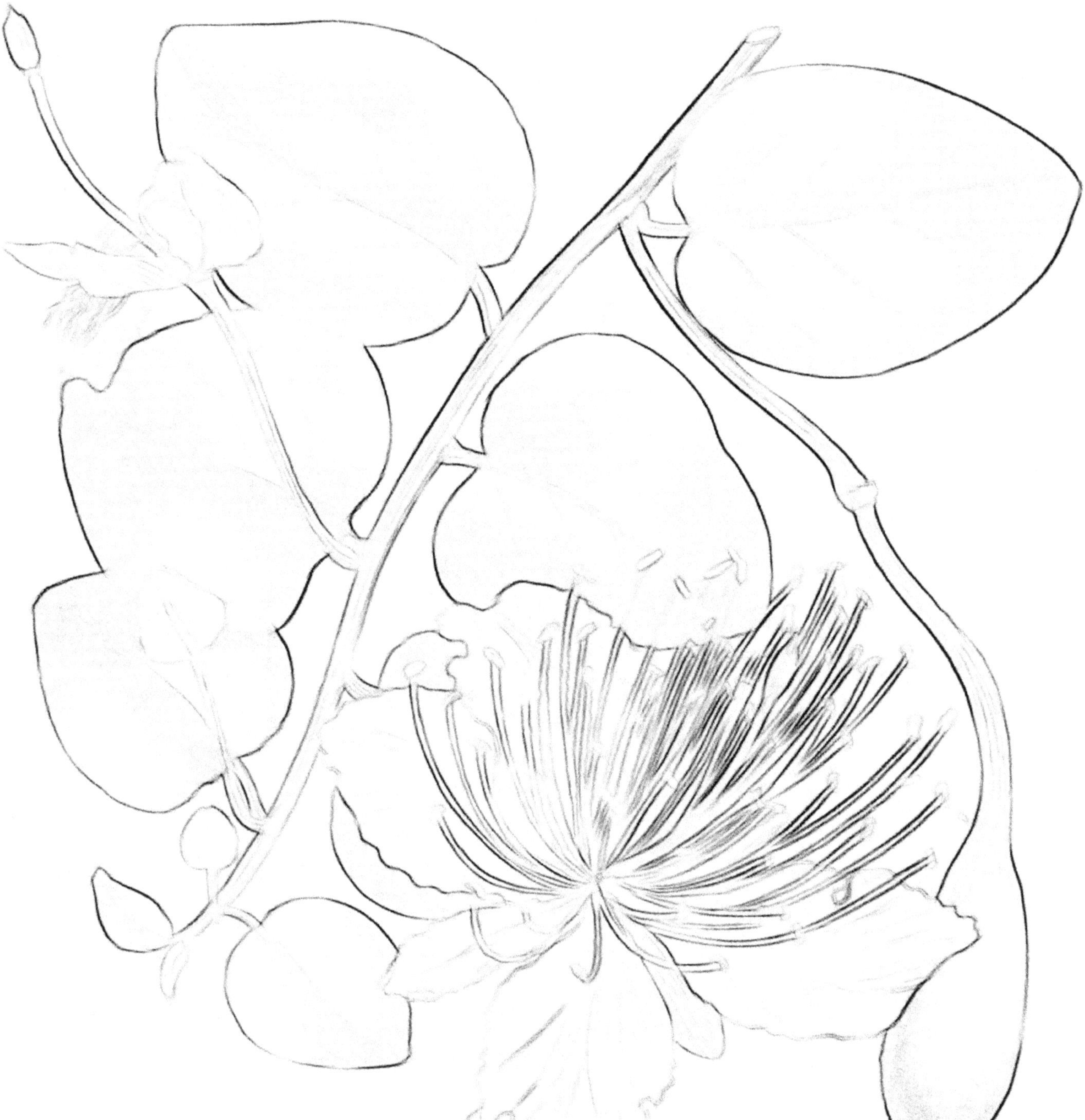

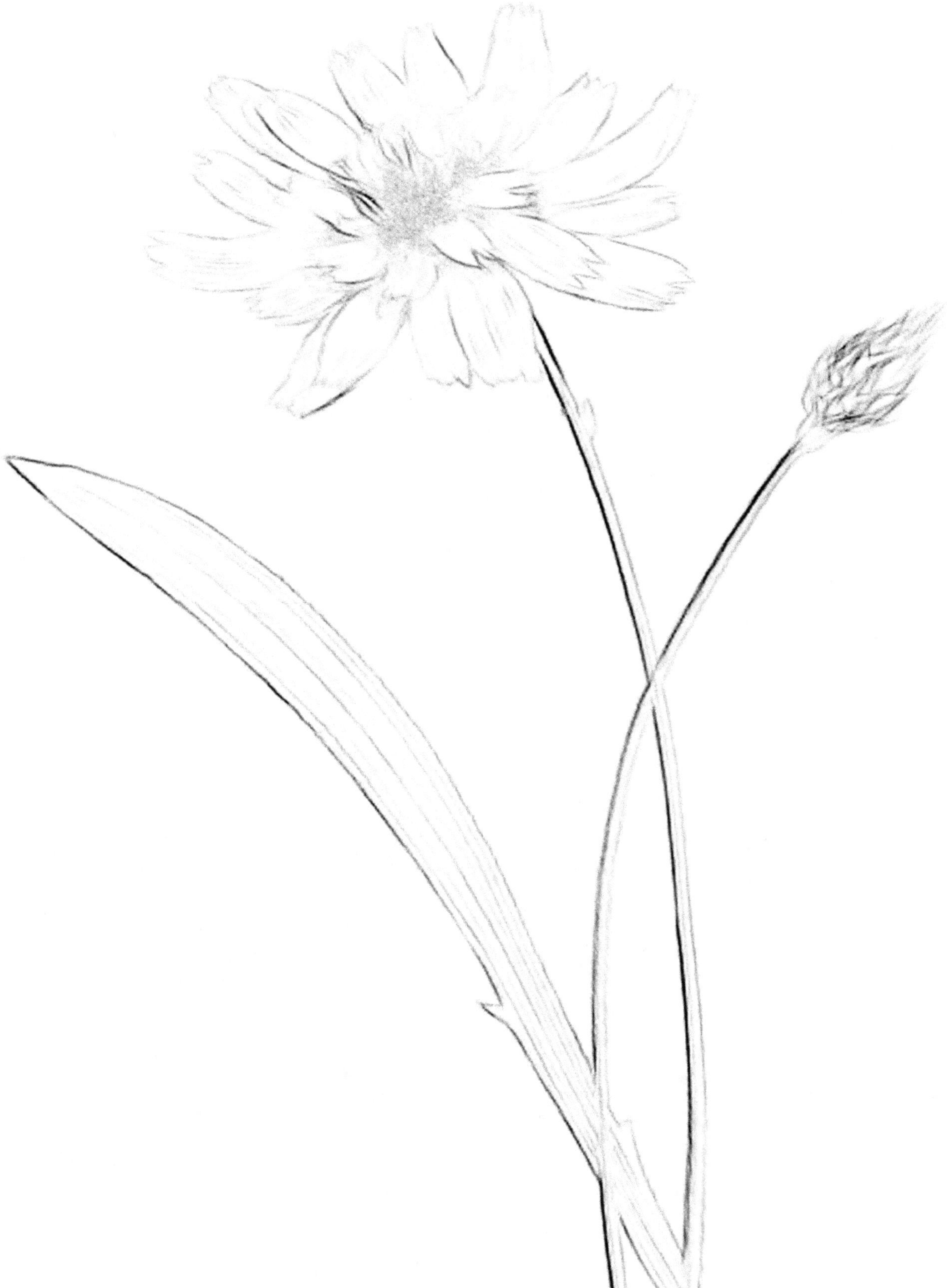

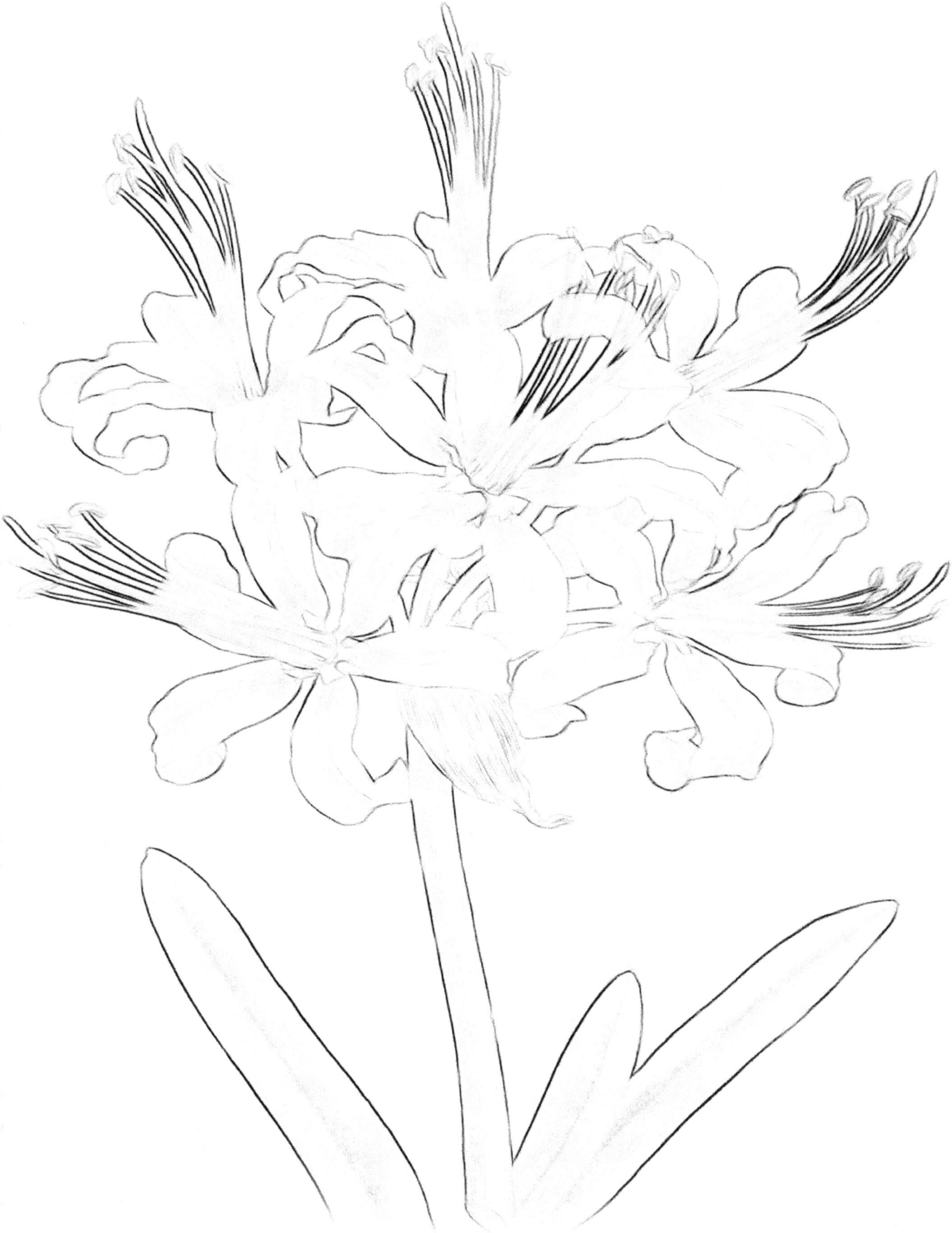

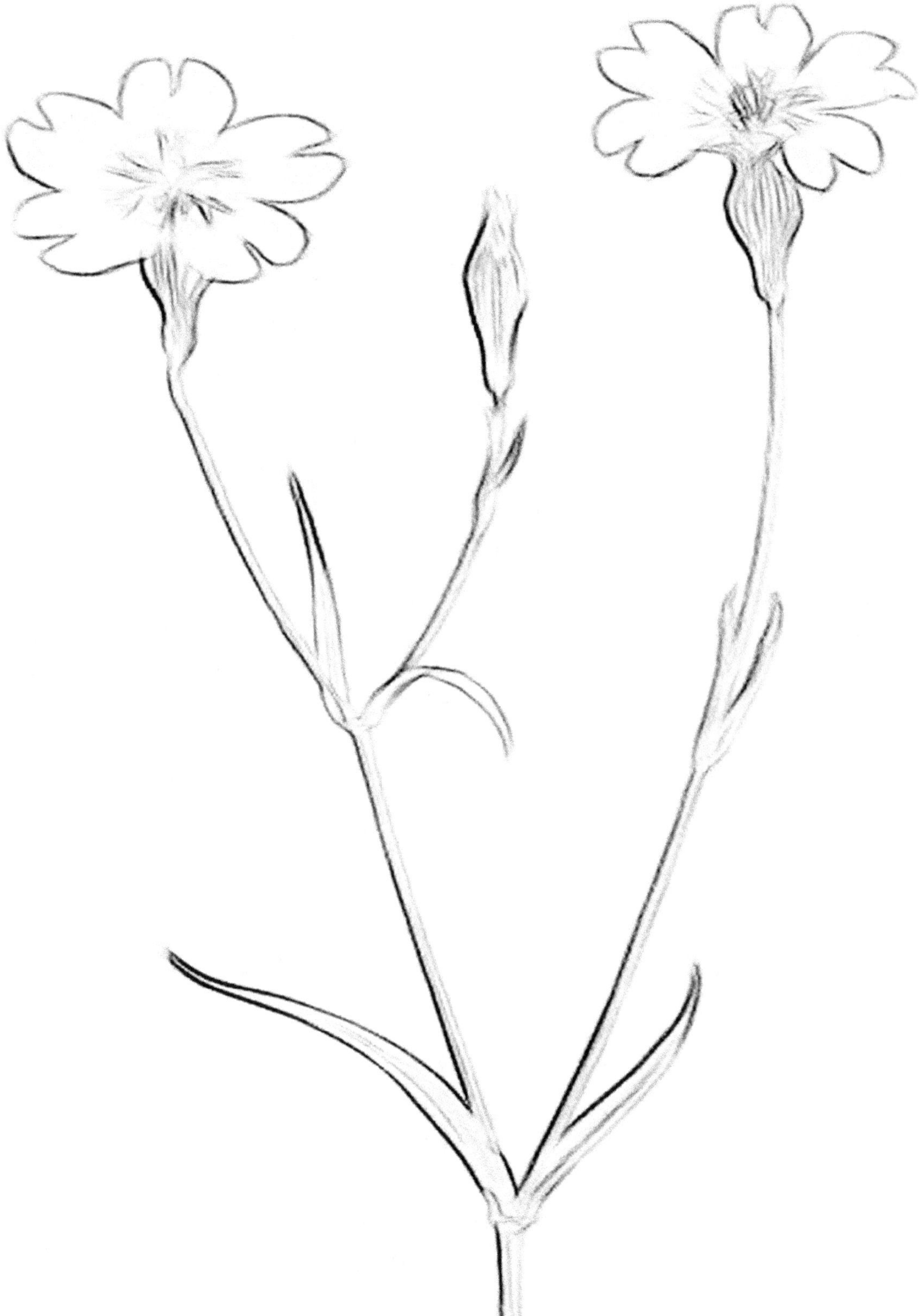

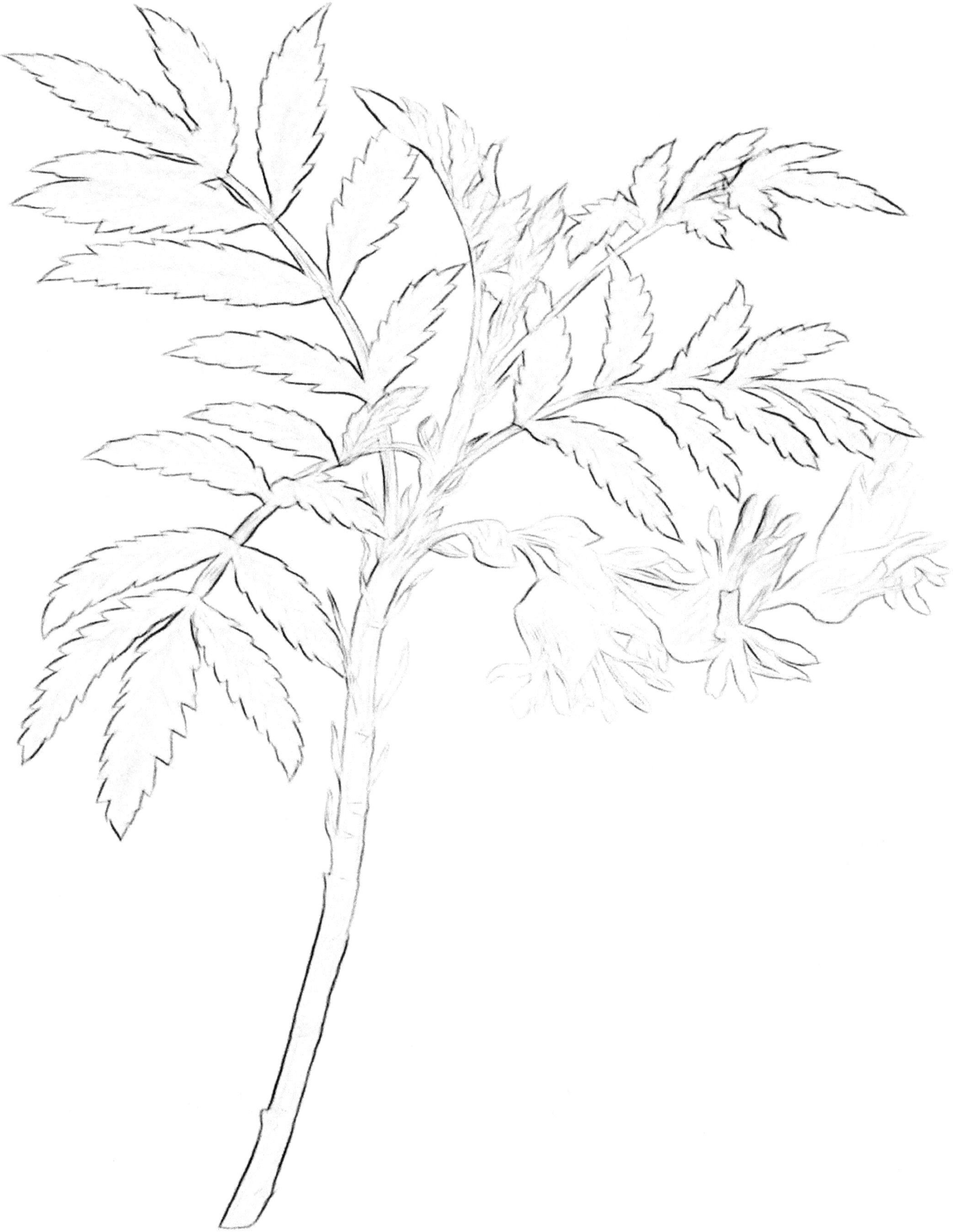

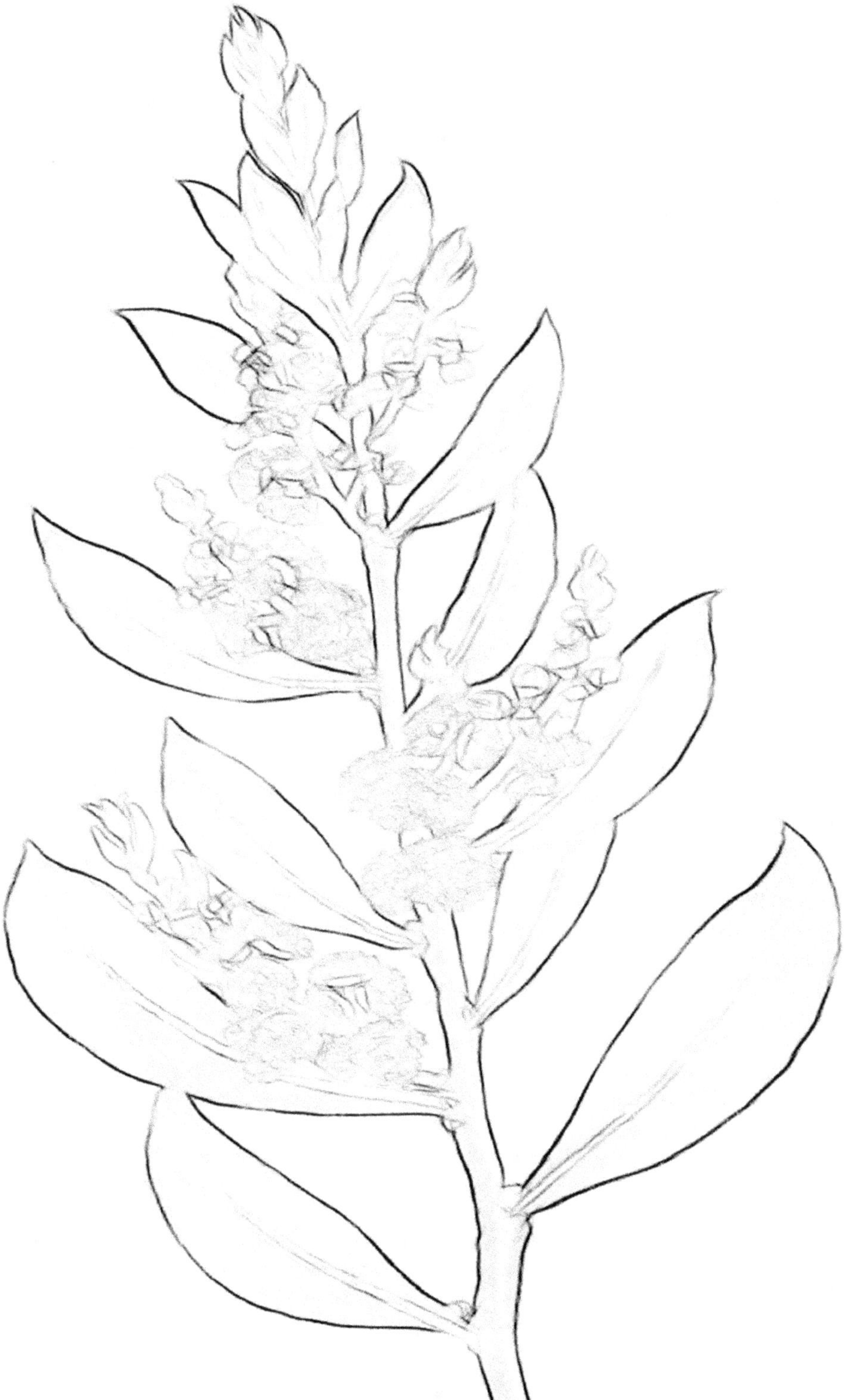

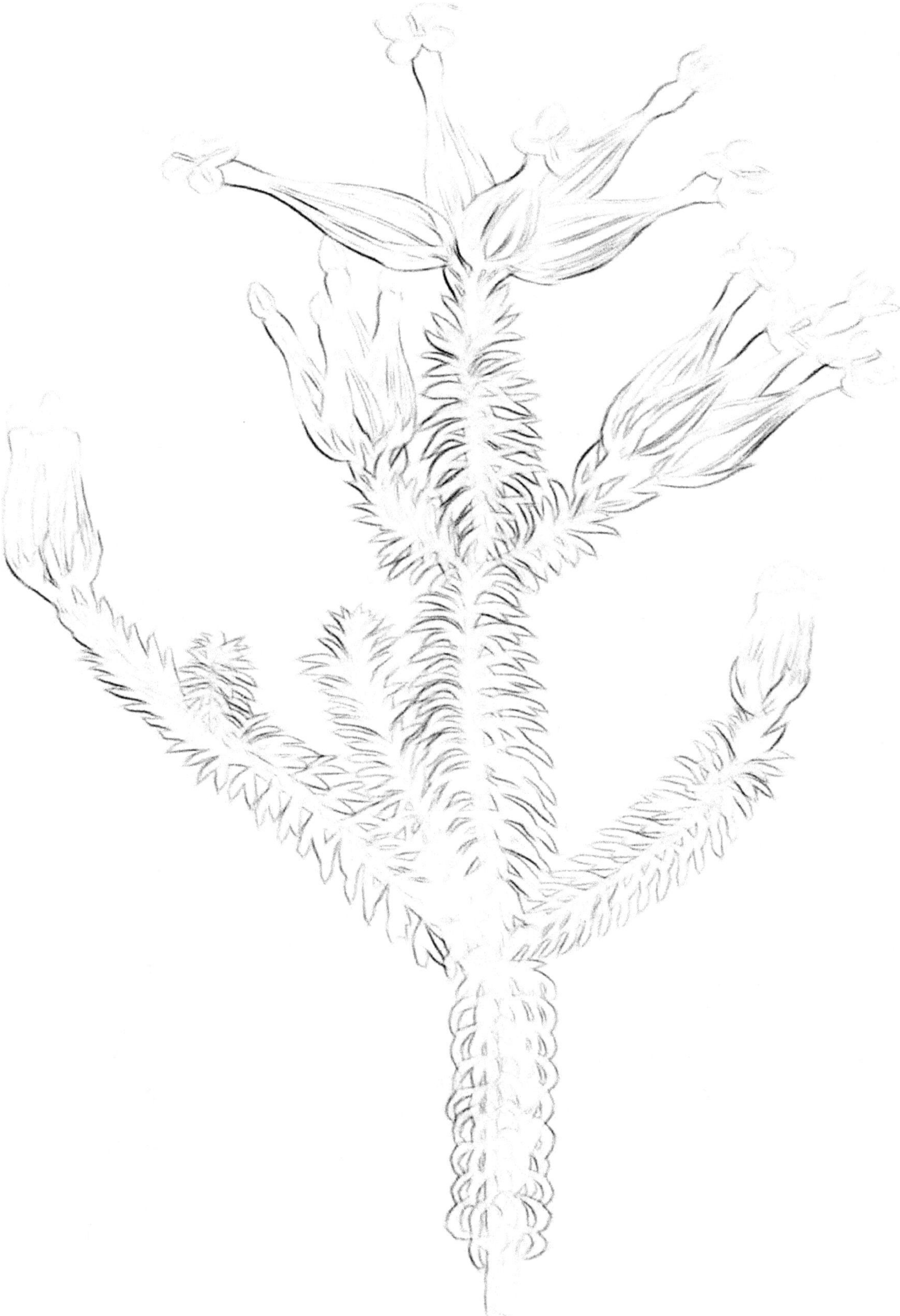

www.ingramcontent.com/pod-product-compliance
Lightning Source LLC
Chambersburg PA
CBHW081621170526
45166CB00009B/3064